Your Superpower is Love

The Science of Heart Coherence

Peggy Polacek

Illustrated by
Sara Williams

Sara Williams, thank you for your
amazing illustrations.

Ginny Loeffler, thank you for editing, and for the
perfect poem photograph with the miraculous,
naturally occurring rainbow.

In loving memory of
Dana Romsdahl

Lili woke up early. After school, Lili and her mom were going camping for the night.

After Lili finished packing, she went to the kitchen for breakfast. Lili's brother and dad were already at the table eating breakfast.

Lili's mom prepared eggs with fresh vegetables from their garden, fresh fruit and homemade whole grain sourdough toast. Lili was too excited to eat anything, but Lili's mom encouraged her to eat before going to school.

30 Trillion cells
Lysosome
Nuclear pore
Nucleolus
Cytoplasm
Centriole

When Lili was at school, it seemed like the day dragged on slowly. Lili's last class was science, where she learned that the human body, on average, has 30 trillion cells. This new information intrigued her! But Lili had a hard time imagining how many 30 trillion cells were, or even what all those cells did! Lili knew when she arrived home, she could ask her mom, a high school science teacher.

When Lili got home, her mom had the car packed for their overnight camping trip.

Lili's mom said, "Lili, there is a healthy snack ready for you in the kitchen. After you eat your snack, we can leave for our camping trip."

When Lili and her mom got in the car, Lili said, "Mom, today in science class I learned that on average, the human body has 30 trillion cells."

Lili's mom said, "I know Lili, the human body is miraculous. Science demonstrates at conception, your cells are super charged with a spark of light, and designed to work in harmony, be healthy, and radiate love!"

"Lili, when you quiet the mental chatter in your mind, including any emotional unrest inside and outside of yourself, you can connect to the love and harmony in your heart."

Lili said, "I don't understand Mom, what do you mean?"

Lili's mom said, "Lili, you know when you have a fight with your friends or brother, or when you are afraid or anxious, and afterward, you have a headache and a stomachache?"

"The science of Psychoneuroimmunology demonstrates that negative thoughts, feelings and emotions cause most stress, illness and life problems. This science demonstrates that thoughts, feelings and emotions directly affect the nervous and immune systems. Thoughts, feelings and emotions also affect behavior and, thus, life outcomes."

Lili's mom continued, "Lili, the science of heart coherence demonstrates that when you quiet your mind and tune into your heart, you will have more physical energy, your intuition will be stronger, you will be more creative, experience more synchronicities in your life, and awaken and live your divine potential with greater ease."

"You will also be able to handle difficult and awkward situations easily, and have healthier and more harmonious relationships."

Lili said, "That sounds good, Mom. I don't like fighting with my friends or brother. It makes me sad, and I always feel sick afterward."

E=mc²

Lili's mom continued, "Lili, the scientific study of epigenetics demonstrates you can alter or change the expression of your DNA through the choices you make in your environment. This includes the influences of environmental toxins, EMFs (electromagnetic radiation fields), your stress level, what you eat, ingest and inject into your body. It also includes how much exercise and sleep you get, your thoughts, beliefs, feelings and emotions. Lili, the science demonstrates that your choices not only affect you, but your offspring too."

"Lili, I love teaching this science to students because it is so empowering to know that you can maintain a healthy mind, body and spirit through self-discipline, and by the healthy choices you make."

"Lili, it is miraculous that you were born with God frequency in every cell of your physical being. The science of heart coherence demonstrates that when your heart is centered in love, it becomes your superpower. You are less vulnerable to other people's negative influence; you have stronger intuition which results in better decisions; and overall, a healthier life: physically, emotionally and spiritually."

Lili and her mom finally arrived at their camp site and set up camp. After the tent was set up and everything was in place, they continued their conversation.

Lili asked, "Mom, what can I do to connect to my heart's superpower?"

Lili's mom said, "Lili, it is important to take personal responsibility and *ACT*, which means you need to self-regulate your thoughts, feelings, emotions and actions. First, you must become *Aware* of your thoughts, feelings, emotions and actions. When you know how you are feeling, you can process those feelings and make healthy *Choices*. One way to do this is by using empowering and healthy *Tools* so your heart can stay in the vibration of divine love."

"*ACT* means becoming *Aware*, making good *Choices*, and utilizing healthy *Tools*. It means being mindful of what you think, feel, say and do."

"Lili, you are innately empowered to self-regulate and be loving, joyful, healthy, creative and productive."

"Lili, let's go on a nature walk and discuss how you can accomplish this."

Lili and her mom started walking on a nearby path. Lili's mom said, "Lili, science demonstrates that being in nature has profound physical, emotional and spiritual health benefits. Spending time in nature connects you to your heart center, lowers stress levels, helps with self-regulation, increases energy, reduces inflammation, lowers chronic pain, improves sleep, lessens depression and anxiety, and improves overall health and well-being."

"Lili, to connect to your heart's superpower, it is important to take care of your physical body and all 30 trillion cells you learned about in science class today. Also, tending to your feelings and emotions, and nurturing the divine spirit of love within you is essential."

"Lili, you can accomplish this by spending more time in nature, eating a healthy diet, drinking plenty of clean water, exercising and getting a good night's sleep. Also, you need to be aware of and process your feelings and emotions in a healthy manner."

"Lili, nature was created to provide for your needs. See the wild asparagus growing over there? The food, herbs and spices that farmers or individuals grow are nature's medicine. Lili, it is important to eat a healthy diet with a variety of fresh vegetables and fruits, whole grains, herbs, spices, healthy fats, nuts, seeds, legumes and other healthy proteins. It's also important to eat a variety of fermented foods. Lili, fermented foods have good bacteria in them. They support a healthy immune system, can improve your gut, brain, other organs and mental health. Fermented food can reduce your risk of cardiovascular disease, high blood pressure, diabetes, inflammation and obesity."

Lili's mom continued walking down the path as Lili skipped slightly ahead. Lili's mom said, "Lili, let's stop for a moment and feel the warm rays of the sun shining on us."

After Lili paused to feel the sun's rays, she said, "Mom, the sun feels warm and comforting."

Lili's mom replied, "I agree Lili, the sun feels so good. Lili, sunlight is very important to your health. Sunlight provides your body with vitamin D, which is crucial for a healthy immune system. Also, exposure to sunlight helps your brain release a hormone called serotonin. Serotonin helps boost and regulate your mood and emotions, making you feel calm and focused. Serotonin enhances your digestion and controls your appetite, and helps you sleep better. Individuals with low serotonin can have mood disorders and depression."

"Lili, it is easier to live your life connected to your heart's superpower when you are exposed to regular sunlight, eat healthy foods, drink plenty of fresh clean water, exercise, tend to your feelings and get a good night's sleep."

Lili started to skip down the path again and said, "Mom, I am always happy when the sun is shining, and I am playing outside."

As Lili and her mom continued down the path, they saw a family having fun while playing tag in an open field. Lili's mom said, "Lili, to stay healthy you need physical activity. Scientific studies demonstrate that staying physically active strengthens your bones and muscles, which makes you stronger and gives you more energy to accomplish your goals. Studies also show that exercise manages and prevents illness and disease. It helps improve the health of your heart, both physically and emotionally. Exercise helps you sleep better, reduces your stress level, and improves your mood and overall emotional well-being. Exercise controls your blood pressure, helps maintain healthy weight, improves your blood sugar level and helps maintain and improve cognitive function."

Lili said, "Mom, it is amazing there are so many health benefits from an activity that is fun and empowering."

Lili's mom said, "I know Lili, it is so delightful to see how much fun that family is having playing tag together. Your life is designed to be shared with family and friends. Science demonstrates that when you gather with family, friends and community with an open and loving heart, you will be healthier and happier. Your heart, brain and nervous system will be healthier, and you will have less emotional and physical pain. Lili, it is important to learn how to connect to and share the love in your heart, and manage your emotions and behavior, so you don't push love away."*

Lili said, "Mom, some days I feel lazy, and just want to lay around and play video games and watch television, but I always feel better when I am outside with my friends and family."

*Harvard's 75 Year Grant and Glueck Study

Lili and her mom continued down the path as the family's joyful laughter faded into silence. Lili's mom decided to take advantage of the silence and said, "Lili, let's go sit under that tree."

After they got comfortable, Lili's mom said, "Lili, you were born with a spark of divine love in every cell of your being. The energy center for your divine spirit is in the center of your chest, near your physical heart. It is your responsibility to make choices that nurture the vibration of love in your relationships, and all life experiences. Because there is so much fear and chaos in this world, it is important to turn *off* your cell phone, television and computer, and make time every day to be still, and align with the divine presence within your heart center."

"Lili, close your eyes and let's participate in a heart coherence technique.* Now, quiet your mind so you can tune into your heart. A good way to do that is to focus on the breath going in and out of your heart center. You can put your hand over your heart, if that helps you."

"Now, inhale a breath for 5 seconds, and exhale for 5 seconds. As you inhale and exhale, experience the feeling of love in your heart center. You can do this by thinking about someone you love, or by thinking about a special place you love to visit or, simply, by focusing on the feeling of love. Let's continue for a couple minutes in silence, Lili."

After several minutes, Lili's mom opened her eyes and could sense that Lili was in a peaceful, calm state. She noticed the sun was starting to set, and knew they needed to finish the meditation and head back to camp to make supper.

*HeartMath Institute

Lili's mom said, "Lili, open your eyes when you are ready." Lili slowly opened her eyes and appeared calm and refreshed. Lili's mom said, "Lili, let's head back to camp. While we are eating supper, we can talk about how you felt during the heart coherence meditation." Lili felt the urge to give her mom a hug and did so.

As the sun started to set, Lili and her mom followed the path back to camp and fixed a healthy supper of homemade vegetable soup, fruit, a mixture of nuts, and fresh homemade wholegrain sourdough bread with walnut butter and honey. Lili's mom brought plenty of filtered water from home and poured some for both of them.

After Lili's mom built a fire to warm up the soup and to stay warm, Lili and her mom sat down to eat. They were both hungry and ate their first few bites in silence.

After eating several bites of her supper, Lili said, "Mom, when I was doing the heart coherence meditation, I felt like I was hugged. I also felt like my heart wanted to give you that big hug."

"Lili, thank you so much for your hug, and for sharing your love with me. It made me feel good."

"Lili, the science of Neurocardiology demonstrates when you do the heart coherence exercise, your heart rhythm beats in coherence. Coherence means your heart is in harmony, and all is well."

"Lili, your heart then sends a harmony signal to your brain, telling your brain that all is well. Then your brain sends a harmony signal to all 30 trillion cells in your body, telling your cells and your entire body, all is well."

"Lili, the more you connect to your heart center in love, the happier, healthier and more productive you will be."

Lili said, "Mom, thank you for having me try the heart coherence exercise. It helped me experience what you are teaching me today."

Lili and her mom finished their supper and enjoyed the fire in silence.

After spending time in silence and observing the stars, Lili's mom said, "Lili, let's clean up and go into our tent and get ready for bed."

Lili said, "I am so excited mom; I love sleeping in a tent."

After Lili and her mom got settled in their tent, they crawled into their sleeping bags. Lili's mom said, "Lili, I have another wellness tool I want to share with you before we go to sleep."

Lili was getting tired, but she wanted to hear what her mom had to say, so she listened closely.

"Lili, all human beings are exposed to hurtful comments, actions and events in their life. Many times, their emotions are not processed and released; they are held deep within their hearts. Carrying hurtful emotions in their heart, Lili, is very damaging to their physical, emotional and spiritual health. It is very common for people to start believing the hurtful words or actions and develop negative self-talk or negative beliefs about themselves."

"Lili, you are a divine spirit having a human experience. You are loved, and you are never alone. When you connect to your heart center, you will begin to know and live that truth. You can use a tool called Self-Affirmations. You can replace the hurtful thoughts, feelings and actions with the truth of who you are."

Lili said, "I love that, mom! How do I use affirmations to be healthier?"

"Lili, it is very simple and empowering. You can say the affirmation in your mind, like a silent prayer, or you can say the affirmation out loud. I do both, depending on where I am when I am using self-affirmations. The key is to say the affirmation with an elevated positive emotion, believing and knowing what you are saying is already so."

"Since you and I are alone now, let's practice doing it out loud. I will say an affirmation, and you can repeat it for yourself or create a different one. We can take turns, Lili. I will start."

I am loved
I am loved

Lili's mom said, "I am loved."

Lili repeated, "I am loved."

Lili's mom said, "I am strong and healthy."

Lili repeated, "I am strong and healthy."

Lili's mom said, "I am divinely empowered to create a happy, healthy, productive life."

Lili repeated, "I am divinely empowered to create a happy, healthy, productive life."

Lili's mom said, "Lili, do you want to try and create an affirmation now? I will follow you."

Lili confidently jumped right in, "I am grateful for my family and friends."

Lili's mom repeated, "I am grateful for my family and friends."

Lili said, "I am divinely blessed."

Lili's mom repeated, "I am divinely blessed."

Lili peacefully said, "I am never alone."

Lili's mom said, "I am never alone."

"Great, Lili! Now let's pause and talk about how that made you feel. Talking about how you feel, with an adult that you trust, is another very important wellness tool," Lili's mom said.

"Mom, I feel energized, empowered and happy inside. I feel like I just gave myself a great big hug."

"Lili, science demonstrates that when you utilize Self-Affirmation Theory, you can replace negative or unhelpful thoughts held in your subconscious mind with positive ones to motivate yourself and boost your self-esteem. People who have high self- esteem achieve their goals with greater ease and are happier and healthier."

"Also, the science of Self-Affirmation Theory demonstrates that you can reduce stress, positively change your behavior, improve sleep, reframe threatening experiences, rewire neural pathways, lower rumination (constant negative self-talk), and shift to an optimistic mindset."

Lili's mom glanced over at Lili and could sense she was tired and wanted to go to sleep, so she said, "Lili, let's go to sleep now. Studies demonstrate that getting a good night's sleep is vital for health and well-being. During sleep your immune system repairs and restores itself. Sleep is essential for your physical health and performance, including endurance and strength. It is also critical for your mental health and performance, including your cognition, learning, memory, creativity, perception, motivation, judgement, mood and emotions."

"Lili, it is important to create a regular healthy sleep schedule and an environment that is dark, cool, quiet and technology free. Lili, turn your phone and computer *off* at night. Your sleep time is for repairing, restoring and renewing."

Lili said, "Okay, Mom, I understand. Thank you for a great day. I had so much fun. I love you."

Lili's mom replied, "I love you, Lili. Sleep well."

Lili and her mom woke up early. They had a busy day ahead. They had to take down the tent, pack up the car, and head home for a busy day with Lili's dad and brother. Lili and her brother both had soccer games, and then they were taking their grandparents to supper.

When they finished packing the car, Lili said, "Mom, thank you for taking me camping, and teaching me that I am divinely empowered to be loving, happy, healthy, creative and productive. I can't wait to go to science class and tell my teacher everything you taught me."

"Lili, I had so much fun with you. There is so much more to share with you."

Lili and her mom drove home in silence as they processed and savored the experience of their camping trip.

Be Still and Know

Love is
Divine Wholeness,
A Flowing Current
Love's Essence is
Stillness
Peace
All Knowing!
Infinite
Harmony
Grace
Love's Presence is
Compassion
Joy
Love's Vibration is
Divine Light, Freedom
Love Inspires, Heals
Love is Humble
Kind
Patient
Love Empowers All!
Illuminates Truth, Light
Eternally
Be Still and Know Love's Presence